JAPANESE COOKING

Gail Weinshel Katz

Library of Congress catalog card number: 77-99188
ISBN: 0-517-244861
Published under arrangement with Ottenheimer Publishers, Inc.
Printed in the United States of America.

contents

introduction

Welcome to the adventure of Japanese cooking! Freshness and appropriateness to the season are stressed, and it is important that each dish retain its natural flavor and be served at its peak. Do not overcook!

Fish and rice are traditional staples of the Japanese diet, with meat not quite as popular. There are many, many varieties of fish and seafood in Japan's inland and coastal waters, thus accounting for its popularity.

''Converted'' long-grain rice is already processed and needs no washing or rinsing. Instructions for cooking should be followed to a ''T'', omitting the salt, as Japanese rice is cooked without salt. This will approximate long-grain rice prepared as the Japanese do. Lemon juice will make it whiter. The rice should be fluffy and dry. Don't peek while the rice is cooking!

Vegetables are usually selected for their freshness, and seasonal vegetables are used.

Japanese cooking is very eye-appealing and is served most attractively. The food is arranged ahead of time on individual dishes for each person. Additionally, each person's meal may be arranged on an individual tray or a series of trays for large meals. The three meals in a Japanese home may not vary much. They are just as likely to have soup in the morning for breakfast as for the evening meal.

Sukiyaki(pronounced s'kee ah kee) and Tempura are ''festive'' dishes, more likely to be prepared for company. Experiment with the different variations. They are fun dishes to prepare and to eat.

Desserts as we know them are not served after a Japanese meal. The sweet desserts are usually purchased and served with tea, but fresh fruit, ices, or ice cream are the typical desserts enjoyed after the meal.

Some of the recipes in this book call for grilling on a hibachi (''fire basin''), which is a portable Japanese charcoal grill used indoors or outdoors. Hibachis range in size from tiny individual ones to very large double-grill models. Whatever calls for cooking on a hibachi can be grilled on a regular outdoor (or indoor) grill or even under the broiler in your oven.

In the recipes that do not call for amounts of soy sauce and/or seasoning, use the ingredient in question sparingly at the time of preparation. More can be added, if needed. Some people prefer a more highly seasoned dish with a lot of soy-sauce flavor, and others prefer it more bland. The type of soy sauce used will vary the flavor also. Please use a good-quality soy sauce for best results. The oil used in these recipes is *always* vegetable oil, unless otherwise noted.

I have tried to keep the recipes simple, with ingredients that can be found at your local supermarket or a few that can be purchased at an Oriental or Japanese specialty store.

I hope you enjoy trying these recipes as much as I enjoyed putting this book together.

guide to unusual ingredients

candied or sugared ginger

Sold in cellophane packages or sometimes bottles, available at Oriental speciality stores, or possibly your supermarket.

dashi

A basic fish broth made from dried bonito fish and seaweed. It is the stock used in many dishes. You can purchase bags at Oriental specialty stores containing the ingredients to ''brew'' dashi, or you may substitute chicken broth.

gingerroot

A ''hot'' spice, irregularly shaped, light brown in color. Can be purchased at supermarkets.

mirin

Sweet rice wine or ''sweet sake,'' available at liquor stores and Oriental specialty stores. Sherry sweetened with sugar may be substituted.

miso

Fermented soy-bean paste, available in white or the more flavorful red. Can be purchased at Oriental specialty stores.

sake

Japanese rice wine. Available at liquor stores or Oriental specialty stores. Sherry may be used as a substitute. If sake is to be served for drinking, it is served warm.

savory cabbage

A small, light-green cabbage with heavily veined leaves. Can be found at some supermarkets or in Oriental specialty stores with a produce department. Regular cabbage may be used as a substitute.

soy sauce

A dark-colored liquid used in most Oriental recipes. Made from soy beans, wheat, and salt. Can be purchased in bottles at supermarkets. Will keep indefinitely.

appetizers

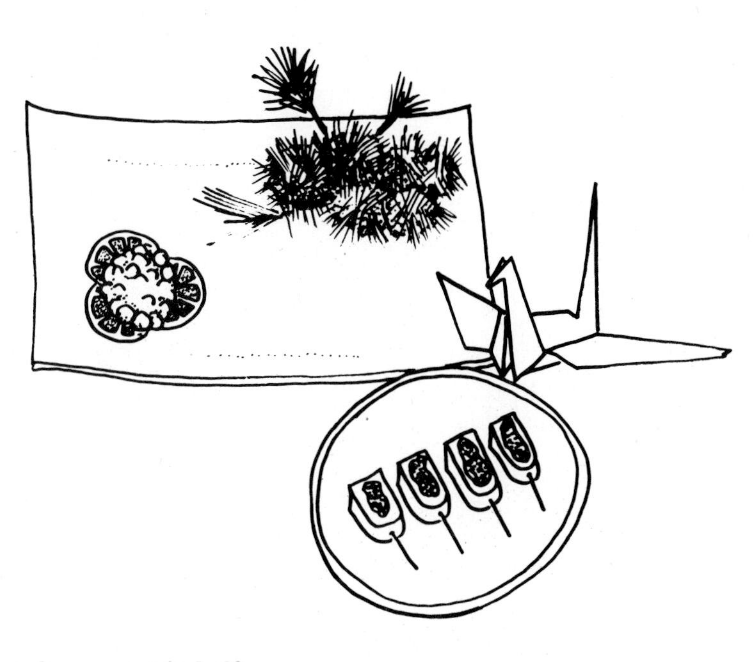

appetizers wrapped in bacon

8 slices bacon, cut in half
1 pound chicken livers, halved
1 6-ounce can whole water chestnuts, drained and sliced

Lay bacon slices flat, place chicken livers and water chestnuts on top, and roll up. Secure with toothpicks.

Place appetizers in small amount of hot oil in frying pan or wok; cook until bacon is browned. Makes 4 servings.

shrimp wrapped in bacon

8 cleaned shrimp with tails intact
8 slices bacon

Wrap shrimp with bacon; fasten with toothpicks. Bake in 350°F oven for 15 to 20 minutes. Serve as an appetizer. Makes 4 servings.

simple fish appetizer

1 6-ounce can tuna
1 teaspoon soy sauce (more, if desired)
2 tablespoons chopped onion

Drain tuna. Mix with soy sauce and chopped onion; spread on rice crackers (or another cracker of your choice) as an appetizer. Makes approximately 5 to 6 servings.

skewered fish meat

6 pieces white fish meat, each about 2 ounces
Salt
7 ounces white miso (soybean paste)
½ cup rice wine (or sherry)
2 tablespoons sugar

Sprinkle fish meat lightly with salt; refrigerate for 12 hours.

Mix soybean paste, rice wine (or sherry), and sugar together until well-blended.

Drain fish, place in mixture, and refrigerate for 24 hours.

Thread fish on skewers; broil in oven, on grill, or on a hibachi. Serve as an appetizer. Makes 3 servings.

fried chicken balls

½ large onion, chopped
1 pound chicken, chopped finely
1 tablespoon sugar
1½ tablespoons mirin (sweet rice wine)
2 tablespoons soy sauce
1 egg
2 tablespoons oil
3½ tablespoons water
1½ tablespoons sherry

Soak chopped onion in water; squeeze out moisture.

Combine chicken and onion with sugar, mirin (or sherry mixed with sugar: 1 part sugar to 2 parts sherry), 1 tablespoon soy sauce, and egg. Stir until thoroughly mixed. Roll into bite-size balls.

Heat oil in pan; brown meatballs on all sides.

Combine water, sherry, and remaining 1 tablespoon soy sauce. Add to meat in pan; cook until liquid is almost evaporated. Makes 4 servings.

chicken liver teriyaki

These make tasty appetizers.

Chicken livers, as many as are needed
Equal amounts of soy sauce, sugar, and water
Soy sauce or mustard for dipping

Marinate livers in mixture of soy sauce, sugar, and water.

Skewer the livers; place on hibachi or grill, turning while cooking.

When done, dip livers into soy sauce or mustard and enjoy. Makes approximately 4 livers per person.

roast beef with horseradish

Horseradish, freshly grated or bottled
Water
4 slices roast beef, each about 1/8 inch thick

Mix horseradish with small amount of water until of spreading consistency. Spread beef with horseradish; roll it up.

Serve as an appetizer. Spread horseradish as thick or thin as you prefer. Makes 2 servings.

beef roll-ups

Ground ginger
2 teaspoons soy sauce
8 ounces thinly sliced lean beef
½ carrot
1 scallion
1 pimiento
2 fresh mushrooms
2 tablespoons oil
2 tablespoons soy sauce
2 tablespoons mirin (sweet rice wine)

Mix a small amount of ginger with 2 teaspoons of soy sauce. Put beef in the mixture; let stand for 20 minutes.

Cut the carrot, scallion, and pimiento into thin slices. Slice the mushrooms thin also.

Lay the beef out flat and fill it with the vegetables. Roll up the beef; fasten it with toothpicks.

Heat oil in skillet. Fry the beef rolls, turning on all sides. Add 2 tablespoons soy sauce and the mirin; turn heat higher for 1 minute.

Remove toothpicks and cut roll-ups into bite-size pieces. If desired, garnish with lettuce leaves.

If you do not have mirin, you can use sherry mixed with sugar: 1 part sugar to 2 parts sherry. Makes approximately 2 servings.

soups

japanese meatball soup

½ pound ground beef or pork
2 eggs
1 tablespoon flour
2 teaspoons freshly grated ginger or 1 teaspoon ground ginger
5 cups beef or chicken stock
1 teaspoon soy sauce
Pinch of salt
3 carrots, parboiled and sliced ¼ inch thick
Very thin spaghetti, enough for 4 small servings, cooked and drained
4 sprigs of parsley

Mix together beef or pork, eggs, flour, and ginger. Set aside.

Mix the stock with the soy sauce and salt. Bring to a boil. Add the carrots.

Make very small meatballs from the meat mixture, drop gently into the boiling soup, and boil gently for about 15 minutes.

Divide the spaghetti into 4 individual bowls; add the soup and meatballs. Garnish with parsley. Makes 4 servings.

japanese vegetable soup

2 ounces dried mushrooms
Cold water
½ pound lean pork
1 carrot
4 ounces canned bamboo shoots
2 celery stalks
4 cups hot beef broth
4 ounces fresh spinach
3 tablespoons rice wine or sherry
1 tablespoon soy sauce
⅛ teaspoon ground ginger
3 drops Tabasco sauce

Soak mushrooms in a generous amount of cold water for 30 minutes, covering the bowl.

Cut pork into very thin strips.

Cut the carrot and bamboo shoots into matchstick-size pieces.

Cut the celery into thin slices.

Drain the mushrooms; cut them into halves or quarters, depending on size.

Bring beef broth to a boil. Add pork, mushrooms, and other vegetables. Cook over low heat for 10 minutes.

Meanwhile, thoroughly wash the spinach; chop it coarsely.

Remove soup from heat, add spinach, and let stand for 3 minutes. Season soup with rice wine (or sherry), soy sauce, ginger, and Tabasco sauce. Return it to heat; heat through, but do not boil again.

Serve soup in preheated soup bowls or cups. Makes 4 servings.

chicken and vegetable balls

12 ounces leftover cooked chicken, chopped
2 bamboo shoots, cut into very thin strips
4 mushrooms, chopped
2 small carrots, chopped fine
1 egg, beaten
1 teaspoon soy sauce
1 teaspoon sugar
3 cups chicken stock
4 tablespoons soy sauce
1 tablespoon sugar

Combine chicken, bamboo shoots, mushrooms, carrots, egg, 1 teaspoon soy sauce, and 1 teaspoon sugar. Form into balls after mixing very well.

Drop meatballs into the boiling chicken stock to which 4 tablespoons soy sauce and 1 tablespoon sugar have been added. Simmer about 8 minutes.

Serve meatballs hot or cold. The chicken-stock mixture is also served hot poured into individual bowls. Makes 2 servings.

fondue-pot japanese-style chicken soup

½ uncooked boned chicken breast
8 fresh mushrooms
4 cups hot chicken broth
1 cup cooked rice
4 strips lemon peel

Cut chicken meat into thin slices.

Wash and cut mushrooms into thin slices.

Put chicken broth in fondue pot over medium-high heat, add chicken and mushrooms, and cook for 4 minutes.

Place ¼ cup of rice in each of 4 bowls; put 1 lemon-peel strip in each bowl. Spoon in the chicken-broth mixture and enjoy. Makes 4 servings.

chicken soup

5 cups chicken broth
1 4-ounce can mushroom stems and pieces, or slices (drain and reserve liquid)
2 teaspoons soy sauce
1 cup cooked fine noodles
1 chicken breast, cooked, boned, and thinly sliced
4 thin slices lemon with rind

Bring chicken broth to a boil. If there is not 5 cups of broth, add mushroom liquid to make 5 cups. Simmer, covered, for 5 minutes. Add mushrooms; heat through. Add soy sauce and noodles. Stir well; heat for 3 minutes.

Divide sliced chicken equally into 4 bowls. Pour soup into bowls. Garnish each with a lemon slice. Makes 4 servings.

rice chowder

2 cups diced leftover cooked chicken
5 cups chicken stock
2 tablespoons soy sauce
2 tablespoons sherry
Pinch of salt
½ teaspoon ground ginger
4 cups leftover rice
4 chopped scallions

Add diced chicken to the boiling stock that has been mixed with the soy sauce, sherry, salt, and ginger. Simmer slowly for about 10 minutes. Add the leftover rice; heat through.

Put ¼ of the chopped scallions into each of 4 individual bowls. Pour in the soup; serve. Makes 4 servings.

clear soup
suimono

This is a nice soup to start off with before enjoying a dinner of Sukiyaki or Tempura.

4 cups chicken broth
1 teaspoon soy sauce
1 teaspoon sugar
Pinch of salt
1 cup cubed chicken
1 scallion, chopped fine
Few sprigs of parsley

Combine chicken broth, soy sauce, sugar, and salt; bring to a boil. In each of 4 bowls put a few cubes of chicken, a few pieces of scallion, and parsley for garnish. Pour soup into bowls; serve without spoons. Makes 4 servings.

egg-flower soup with water chestnuts

1 quart chicken broth
½ cup finely chopped water chestnuts
2 eggs, beaten
¼ teaspoon pepper

Bring chicken broth to a boil. Add water chestnuts, cover, and simmer for 4 minutes. Add beaten eggs slowly while stirring soup. Add pepper; stir through once. Makes 6 servings.

miso soup with egg

4 cups chicken broth
¼ cup white miso (soybean paste)
¼ teaspoon salt
1 egg, beaten
2 teaspoons sherry or sweet rice wine (sweet sake)
Lemon-peel twists

Bring broth, miso, and salt to a boil. While slowly mixing the soup, gradually pour in the egg. Remove from heat; stir in the sherry or sake. Place a twist of lemon peel in each bowl before adding soup. Makes 4 servings.

japanese clam soup

16 small clams
4 cups boiling water
½ teaspoon salt
¾ teaspoon rice wine or sherry
1 tablespoon soy sauce
Lemon slices for garnish

Thoroughly wash the clams. Put them into boiling water; boil them until the shells crack. Put in the salt, rice wine or sherry, and soy sauce. Serve the clam soup with a garnish of lemon slice. Makes 4 servings.

lobster soup

6 ounces lobster meat
2¼ teaspoons salt
1½ teaspoons soy sauce
4½ cups dashi
2 medium cucumbers, sliced thin
8 dried mushrooms
4 pieces lemon rind

Mince the lobster meat, pour ½ teaspoon of the salt over it, and boil. Gradually add ¾ teaspoon of soy sauce and ¼ cup of dashi to the lobster.

Peel and slice the cucumbers.

Boil the mushrooms in ¼ cup of dashi and ¾ teaspoon of salt.

Into each of 4 bowls place pieces of boiled lobster, cucumbers, and mushrooms.

Heat together 4 cups of dashi, ¾ teaspoon of salt, and ¾ teaspoon of soy sauce; pour some into each bowl.

Garnish lobster soup with floating lemon rind. Makes 4 servings.

oyster soup

8 ounces shucked oysters
4 cups dashi
¾ teaspoon cornstarch
Small amount of cold water
½ teaspoon Tabasco

Wash the oysters. Add them to the boiling dashi; cook until the oysters are done.

Mix the cornstarch with enough cold water to make a smooth paste; add to soup. Flavor with the Tabasco. Makes 4 servings.

oyster soup with miso

8 ounces shucked oysters
3½ ounces miso (soybean paste)
4 cups dashi
¾ teaspoon cornstarch
Cold water
½ teaspoon red pepper

Wash oysters; set aside.

Blend the miso and dashi; bring to a boil. Gradually add oysters to the boiling mixture.

Mix the cornstarch with enough cold water to make a smooth paste; add this to the oyster mixture, stirring constantly. Simmer until done. Flavor with red pepper. Makes 4 servings.

salads

japanese salad

1 large cucumber
2 carrots
1 large white radish
Salt
½ pound fresh mushrooms
10 ounces fresh shrimp
2 tablespoons chopped parsley
1 tablespoon chopped fresh dill

salad dressing
2 eggs
Salt
Pinch of sugar
3 tablespoons melted butter
2 tablespoons wine vinegar
1 teaspoon paprika

garnish
1 peach, sliced
1 mandarin orange or 1 tangerine, sectioned
½ orange, sliced

Grate unpeeled cucumber, carrots, and radish. Sprinkle with salt; let stand for 30 minutes. Drain off as much liquid as possible.

Thinly slice mushrooms; mix with vegetables. Add shrimp and chopped fresh herbs. Toss; set aside for 15 minutes.

Meanwhile, prepare dressing by placing eggs, salt, sugar, and melted butter in top of double boiler. Beat over hot water until creamy. Remove from heat. Gradually add vinegar, beating constantly until dressing has cooled off. Season to taste with paprika.

Pour dressing over salad. Garnish with peach slices, mandarin orange or tangerine sections, and orange slices. Makes 6 servings.

quick-and-easy salad

1 large cucumber, sliced
2 scallions, sliced in 1-inch pieces

salad dressing
1½ teaspoons soy sauce
2½ tablespoons sugar
6 tablespoons vinegar

Slice cucumber (do not peel).

Slice scallions; toss with cucumber.

Mix together soy sauce, sugar, and vinegar. You may want to adjust the amounts to suit your taste.

Pour dressing over vegetables. Toss well; serve. If you desire, you can sprinkle a few sesame seeds on top. Makes 2 servings.

ellen's marinated bean sprouts

This is an excellent salad to serve with meat or fish. It has a unique flavor. Try it for guests who like to sample something a little unusual. It's a favorite of ours!

1 pound fresh bean sprouts

marinade
3 tablespoons chopped scallion (use green and white parts)
2 tablespoons sesame-seed oil
2 tablespoons soy sauce
1 tablespoon vodka
1 tablespoon vinegar

Place bean sprouts in colander; blanch. Immediately rinse them with cold water; drain well.

Combine remaining ingredients in a large bowl.

Place bean sprouts in mixture to marinate at room temperature for 1 hour. Refrigerate for at least 3 hours before serving. Makes 4 servings.

cucumber salad

3 medium cucumbers

marinade
⅓ cup white-rice vinegar
4 teaspoons sugar
1 teaspoon salt
Fresh gingerroot to taste, finely chopped

Peel (optional) cucumbers; cut them in half lengthwise. Remove large seeds; slice crosswise into thin slices.

Mix together vinegar, sugar, salt, and ginger.

Chill cucumber slices in vinegar marinade for at least 2 hours. Makes 6 servings.

Note: White vinegar can be substituted for the rice vinegar, but you might want to dilute it with a little water.

japanese egg salad

7½ ounces canned tuna fish
1 can mandarin oranges, approximately 11 ounces
16 stuffed olives
4 hard-boiled eggs

salad dressing
2 tablespoons oil
2 scant tablespoons lemon juice
2 tablespoons soy sauce
Salt
Pepper
Pinch of sugar

Parlsey sprigs for garnish

Drain tuna fish; tear into bite-size pieces with a fork.

Drain mandarin oranges and olives. Slice olives and hard-boiled eggs. Toss all ingredients lightly.

To prepare dressing, combine oil, lemon juice, soy sauce, salt, pepper, and sugar; stir until well-blended.

Pour dressing over salad. Refrigerate for 10 minutes or longer. Divide among 4 individual glass bowls and garnish with parsley sprigs. Makes 4 servings.

cauliflower salad

1 small cauliflower
3 tablespoons peanut butter
Water
Pinch of salt
Chopped peanuts

Boil cauliflower; separate into florets.

Mix peanut butter with water until thin. Season with salt. Mix in with the cauliflower. Sprinkle a little chopped peanuts over the top. Makes 4 servings.

fresh spinach salad

10 ounces fresh spinach
4 ounces fresh mushrooms
¼ cup chopped scallion
Small amount soy sauce
Sesame seeds (optional)

Thoroughly wash spinach; tear up larger pieces. Drain well.

Slice mushrooms; add to spinach. Add chopped scallion; toss well. Sprinkle with the amount of soy sauce desired; toss lightly. Sprinkle each portion with sesame seeds. Makes 4 servings.

rice salad

2 cups water
Salt
4 ounces long-grain rice
1 ounce dried mushrooms
8 ounces bean sprouts, canned or fresh
8 ounces canned bamboo shoots
4 ounces cooked ham
1 medium cucumber
4 tablespoons rice wine or brandy

salad dressing
5 tablespoons oil
5 tablespoons lemon juice
3 tablespoons rice wine or sherry
2 tablespoons soy sauce
Salt

garnish
1 small head Boston lettuce
1 lemon
Salt

Bring salted water to a boil. Add rice; cook for 15 minutes (or use your own method). Place rice in sieve. Pour cold water over it; drain thoroughly.

Chop mushrooms; place in small bowl. Cover with boiling water; let soak for 20 minutes.

Drain bean sprouts, if canned. If using fresh bean sprouts, blanch, rinse with cold water, and drain them.

Drain the bamboo shoots. Cut bamboo shoots into ¼-inch-wide strips.

Cut ham into ¼-inch-wide, 2-inch-long strips.

Cut unpeeled cucumber in half, then into thin slices lengthwise, and finally into 2-inch-long thin strips.

Drain the mushrooms.

To prepare salad dressing, combine oil, lemon juice, rice wine or sherry, soy sauce, and salt to taste; stir until well-blended.

Add rice, bean sprouts, bamboo shoots, ham, cucumber, and mushrooms to dressing; toss thoroughly. Cover; refrigerate for 30 minutes to let flavors blend.

Meanwhile, wash lettuce and pat it dry. Tear it into large pieces. Line a serving platter with it. Arrange rice salad on top.

Cut off both ends of lemon until pulp is visible. Place on platter. Sprinkle top of lemon with salt.

Heat rice wine or brandy, pour it over lemon, and ignite. Serve immediately. (Lemon is only garnish, it is not eaten). Makes 4 servings.

eggs

japanese scrambled eggs

4 fresh mushrooms, sliced
2 scallions, cut into ½-inch pieces
Butter or oil
4 eggs, lightly beaten
Few sprinkles of soy sauce

Slice mushrooms and scallions; sauté in butter or oil for 2 minutes.

Beat eggs, add a few sprinkles of soy sauce, and scramble in skillet with mushrooms and scallions until sufficiently cooked. If desired, add ½ teaspoon sherry to the eggs before cooking. Makes 2 servings.

japanese omelet

4 ounces white fish meat, finely minced
2½ tablespoons flour
½ teaspoon salt
6 eggs, beaten
3 tablespoons sugar
Oil for frying

Mix together fish, flour, and salt. Add beaten eggs; mix well. When thoroughly blended, add sugar.

Heat oil in pan; when hot, pour in egg mixture. Cover; simmer for 15 minutes or until bottom is browned. Turn; cook other side. If desired, sprinkle with finely chopped scallion. Makes 4 servings.

rolled fish omelet

6 ounces white fish such as sole, flounder, etc.
6 eggs, lightly beaten
3 tablespoons soy sauce
3 tablespoons sugar
3 tablespoons water
3 tablespoons mirin or sherry
Salt
Dash freshly ground pepper
Oil

Chop fish fine; mix with eggs, soy sauce, sugar, water, mirin (if sherry is substituted, add 1½ tablespoons more sugar), salt to taste, and pepper. Cook half of this mixture in pan on medium heat, turning to cook both sides. Remove from pan; roll it up like jelly roll. Serve omelet hot. Makes approximately 4 to 5 servings.

zucchini and mushroom omelet

1 zucchini, sliced thin
12 fresh mushrooms, sliced
¼ cup chopped onions
Butter or oil
Salt
Pepper
6 eggs, beaten

Slice zucchini; set it aside.

Slice mushrooms; set them aside.

Chop onions; combine with zucchini.

Heat butter or oil in skillet; sauté the zucchini and onions until just tender. Add the mushrooms; cook for about 30 seconds more. Add salt and pepper to season. Add beaten eggs to mixture in skillet. Cook on medium heat until bottom is browned. Carefully turn omelet, cover, and cook until browned on other side. Makes approximately 4 servings.

chicken and mushrooms in eggs

¼ pound chicken meat
¼ pound fresh mushrooms
2 onions

sauce
½ cup chicken stock
4 tablespoons soy sauce
4 tablespoons rice wine or sherry

4 eggs
4 cups rice

Thinly slice chicken meat, mushrooms, and onions.

Combine the chicken stock, soy sauce, and rice wine or sherry. Bring to boil.

Add chicken, mushrooms, and onions to sauce. Cook this mixture slowly for about 15 minutes.

Place ¼ of the cooked mixture in a small frying pan. Pour a lightly beaten egg over this; cook until almost firm. Remove from pan and serve over rice. This is repeated 3 more times to serve 4 people. Makes 4 servings.

meat

japanese fondue

1 pound beef, cut into cubes
8 ounces hot dogs
4 pimientos
½ pound mushrooms
4 small onions
Oil for deep-frying

sauces
Worcestershire sauce
Lemon juice
Mayonnaise
Catsup

Cut beef into cubes; set aside.

Cut hot dogs into bite-size pieces; set aside.

Cut pimientos into 2 or 3 pieces.

Leave mushrooms whole.

Slice onions into wide rings.

Arrange all ingredients on platter.

Heat oil in fondue pot or wok set on table. Using fondue forks, pick up one ingredient at a time; deep-fry until done.

Eat beef with any of the above sauces. Makes 4 servings.

tasty fondue

bouillon

6 cups chicken bouillon
2 carrots
1 leek
1 stalk celery
2 tablespoons coarsely chopped parsley

sauce tartare

5 tablespoons mayonnaise
2 tablespoons capers
2 tablespoons finely chopped chives
2 dill pickles, finely chopped
2 teaspoons lemon juice
2 tablespoons evaporated milk
Salt
Pinch of sugar
White pepper

catsup sauce

5 tablespoons mayonnaise
2 tablespoons tomato catsup
1 teaspoon Worcestershire sauce
1 teaspoon (or less) curry powder
Pinch of sugar
Salt

2 to 2½ pounds very lean beef
2 cups boiling water

Bring chicken bouillon to a boil either in pot placed on the burner or in fondue pot.

Chop carrots, leek, and celery; add to broth together with chopped parsley. Cook for 20 minutes.

To prepare sauces, stir together ingredients until well-blended. Season to taste.

Thoroughly dry meat with paper towels. Cut into thin strips.

Place chicken—vegetable broth on top of burner; make sure it continues to simmer (or leave in fondue pot over low heat). Since liquid will evaporate, it is necessary to add some of the hot water from time to time.

Each person places a piece of meat on a fonude fork, puts it in simmering broth for 1 to 2 minutes, and dunks it in sauce. Pass to each person his own separate bowl for each of the sauces. Serve with rice. Makes 4 servings.

sweet-and-sour meatballs

1 pound lean ground beef
1 egg, beaten
1 teaspoon (scant) salt
Pepper to taste, freshly ground
1 tablespoon onion flakes
1 tablespoon cornstarch
Oil for frying
1 13½-ounce can pineapple tidbits, drained (reserve liquid)
1 cup water
1 package sweet-and-sour sauce mix
½ cup thinly sliced green pepper

Combine beef, beaten egg, salt, and pepper to taste. Mix in onion and cornstarch. Shape into small-size meatballs.

Brown meatballs in small amount of oil in frying pan or wok. Drain on paper towels. Discard pan drippings. In same pan combine reserved pineapple liquid, water, and sweet –sour mix. Stir constantly until mixture boils. Add green pepper, meatballs, and pineapple. Bring to a boil; turn heat down; simmer for 5 minutes, stirring occasionally.

Serve meatballs on hot rice. Makes 4 servings.

teriyaki meatballs

1 pound lean ground beef
2 tablespoons chopped parsley
2 tablespoons chopped chives
Leaves from 2 stalks of celery, finely chopped
1 egg
3 tablespoons bread crumbs
Salt
White pepper
Butter or margarine for frying

sauce
½ cup soy sauce
Salt
White pepper
Sugar
Monosodium glutamate (MSG)
⅛ teaspoon allspice
Ground ginger
1 sugared ginger

Mix ground beef thoroughly with chopped parsley, chives, and celery leaves. Stir in egg and bread crumbs. Season to taste with salt and pepper. Shape into balls about 1½ to 2 inches in diameter.

Heat butter or margarine in heavy skillet. Add meatballs; fry for about 5 minutes or until browned on all sides.

While meatballs are frying, prepare sauce. In a small saucepan heat soy sauce over low heat. Season with salt, pepper, sugar, MSG, allspice, and ground ginger. Dice sugared ginger; add to sauce.

Pour hot sauce over meatballs; let stand for 5 minutes, so flavors can blend.

Serve meatballs in preheated bowl. Makes 4 servings.

oriental meatballs

These are very tasty meatballs. My family enjoys this recipe very much.

2 pounds lean ground beef
2½ teaspoons salt
⅛ teaspoon freshly ground black pepper
1 egg, beaten
2 tablespoons flour
Small amount freshly ground black pepper
½ cup oil
12 ounces canned chicken broth
3 tablespoons cornstarch
2 to 3 teaspoons soy sauce
½ cup vinegar
½ cup light corn syrup
5 medium green peppers, cut in sixths
8 slices canned pineapple, quartered, or chunks or tidbits
10 maraschino cherries (optional)

Combine beef, 1 teaspoon of the salt, and ⅛ teaspoon pepper. Shape into small meatballs.

Combine egg, flour, ½ teaspoon salt, and a small amount of pepper. Beat until smooth.

Heat oil and remaining 1 teaspoon salt in large frying pan.

Gently place meatballs in batter, 1 or 2 at a time, and fry in the hot oil, browning well on all sides. Remove meatballs from pan. Drain off remaining oil.

Blend ½ cup of the chicken broth with cornstarch. Add remaining chicken broth, soy sauce, vinegar, and corn syrup; cook over medium heat, stirring constantly, until thick and clear. Add green peppers, pineapple, and cherries. Lower heat; cook slowly for about 10 minutes. Pour over meatballs.

Serve meatballs with rice. Makes 6 servings.

eggplant and ground-beef casserole

1 medium to small eggplant
2 eggs, beaten
Bread or cracker crumbs
Oil for frying
1 pound ground beef or veal
Salt
Pepper
Sherry or white wine

Peel eggplant; slice into about ¼-inch slices. Dip into beaten egg, then into bread or cracker crumbs. Fry in heated oil over medium heat until browned; drain on paper towels.

Place a layer of eggplant on bottom of casserole dish.

Discard excess oil from skillet; crumble ground beef or veal into pan; cook until browned, adding salt and pepper to taste. Add a small amount of sherry or white wine to the mixture; place a layer of meat on top of eggplant. Repeat until layers are complete. Makes approximately 3 to 4 servings.

steak japanese

2 filet mignon steaks, about 12 ounces each
2½ tablespoons soy sauce
1 can bean sprouts, or 8 ounces fresh
3 tablespoons butter
2 tablespoons lemon juice
Sugar
Black pepper
4 ounces mandarin oranges (canned)
4 tablespoons oil

Sprinkle 2 tablespoons of the soy sauce over steaks. Rub in; let steaks marinate for 1 hour.

Meanwhile, drain bean sprouts; or, if using fresh bean sprouts, blanch them, rinse with cold water, then drain.

Heat 2 tablespoons of the butter in a saucepan. Add bean sprouts; season with lemon juice, sugar, pepper, and ½ tablespoon soy sauce. Simmer for 5 minutes, then keep them warm.

In another small saucepan heat remaining 1 tablespoon butter, add drained mandarin oranges, and heat through, about 2 minutes. Keep them warm.

In heavy skillet heat oil over high heat until a light haze forms above it. Add steaks; quickly brown them on each side for about ½ minute. Lower heat; continue cooking steaks for about 10 minutes on each side.

Arrange steaks on preheated platter. Garnish with bean sprouts and mandarin oranges. Serve immediately. Makes 2 servings.

oriental pepper steak

1 pound round steak
¼ cup oil
½ teaspoon salt
Pepper to taste
½ cup chopped scallion
2 cloves garlic, chopped fine
4 green peppers, cut into bite-size pieces
1 cup sliced celery
1½ cups beef bouillon
2 tablespoons cornstarch
¼ cup cold water
1 tablespoon soy sauce
Cooked rice

Cut steak into thin slices, then into 2-inch pieces. To make slicing easier, partially freeze the meat.

Heat oil in large skillet. Add salt and pepper. Cook meat over medium to high heat until brown, stirring frequently. Add scallion and garlic. Add green peppers and celery; stir. Add bouillon, cover, and cook until vegetables are tender but still crisp. Do not overcook.

Meanwhile, combine cornstarch and water. Blend in soy sauce until it makes a smooth paste. Slowly add to meat mixture, stirring constantly until liquid is thickened.

Serve steak with rice. Makes 4 servings.

paul's steak encore

This is an excellent "leftover" recipe. Chicken, roast, or any other meat may be used. Try various combinations of vegetables until you hit on the right combination for your family. Use any amount of meat to any amount of vegetables. Some prefer less meat and more vegetables, and others prefer more meat and fewer vegetables. You can use this recipe with any amount of leftover meat.

Steak, leftover cooked
Scallions or onions, chopped
Vegetables:
- **Celery**
- **Green pepper**
- **Cauliflower**
- **Broccoli**
- **Water chestnuts**
- **Bamboo shoots**
- **Peas**
- **Pea pods**

Salt to taste
Freshly ground pepper to taste
Soy sauce to taste

Slice leftover steak very thin. Set aside.

Chop scallions or onions; add to the meat.

Sauté any or all of the above vegetables in heated oil in skillet until just tender. (Pick the vegetables your family is fond of, or other vegetables you have on hand.) When the vegetables are almost done, add the meat and scallions or onions. Just before serving, season to taste with salt, pepper, and soy sauce.

tokyo steak

Delicious with rice and stir-fried bean sprouts.

Salt
Ground ginger to taste
Pepper to taste, freshly ground
2 tablespoons rice wine or sherry
4 filet mignon steaks, about 6 ounces each
1½ tablespoons butter
1 11-ounce can mandarin oranges
1 tablespoon capers
1 tablespoon butter, cut into small pieces

Combine salt, ginger, pepper, and rice wine (or sherry); blend well. Rub mixture onto steaks.

Heat 1½ tablespoons butter in heavy skillet. Add steaks; sauté 2 minutes on each side. Arrange mandarin oranges and capers on top of steaks; dot with remaining 1 tablespoon butter. Place skillet under preheated broiler; broil for 3 minutes.

Serve steaks immediately on preheated plates. Makes 4 servings.

Picture on opposite page: tokyo steak
Picture on next pages: sukiyaki

NIPPON SAKE
NIPPON
THE REFINED JAPANESE SAKE

teriyaki steak

grilled steaks

sukiyaki

1 pound rice
1½ to 2 pounds beef tenderloin
2 tablespoons bacon drippings
½ pound transparent or silver noodles
8 dried mushrooms
4 small onions
4 leeks
¼ head white cabbage (about ½ pound)
½ pound fresh spinach
1 pound canned bamboo shoots
½ pound bean sprouts

sauce
1 cup soy sauce
6 tablespoons rice wine or sherry
2 teaspoons sugar

4 egg yolks

Cook rice according to directions; keep it warm.

Beef tenderloin must be cut into paper-thin slices. To achieve this, place meat in freezer for about 2 hours, or until partially frozen. You then will be easily able to slice it thin. Or, have the butcher slice it for you.

Arrange meat slices on round platter, slightly overlapping. Place 2 tablespoons of bacon drippings (unmelted) into middle, cover with aluminum foil, and refrigerate.

Place noodles and mushrooms into separate bowls. Cover with boiling water; soak for 20 minutes. Repeat procedure two more times. Drain; arrange in separate bowls.

Cut onions and leeks into thin slices. Place in separate bowls.

Core cabbage, separate into individual leaves, and tear into bite-size pieces.

Clean spinach; remove stems from leaves.

Drain bamboo shoots, reserving liquid.

Drain bean sprouts, if canned. If fresh, blanch, then rinse with cold water, and drain them.

To prepare sauce, bring soy sauce, rice wine or sherry, and sugar to a boil. Pour into sauce dish.

Place wok (or use frying pan on top of burner) in the middle of your table. Spoon rice into 4 individual bowls. Place slightly beaten egg yolks into 4 other small bowls. Now arrange all ingredients around wok.

Prepare meal in portions, i.e. place one-fourth of bacon drippings into wok and heat, add one-fourth of meat slices and brown quickly. Push aside and pour some of the sauce over meat. Add one-fourth of each of the vegetables and noodles and simmer for 3 minutes, while stirring constantly.

Each guest is given part of the cooked ingredients and starts eating while the second portion is being prepared. Cooked vegetables are dipped into egg yolk before being placed on plates. Sukiyaki is seasoned with sauce according to each individual's taste. Makes 4 servings.

teriyaki steak

4 boneless steaks, about ½ pound each

marinade

1 clove garlic, finely minced
1 sugared or candied ginger, finely minced
1 tablespoon brown sugar
Salt
Pepper, freshly ground
Pinch of monosodium glutamate (MSG)
½ cup rice wine or sherry
6 tablespoons soy sauce
½ cup white wine
Juice of half a lemon

stuffed-tomato garnish

4 medium tomatoes
Salt
White pepper
4 tablespoons bean sprouts, canned or fresh
1 tablespoon tomato catsup

Combine marinade ingredients in shallow dish large enough to hold the steaks. Stir until well blended.

Add steaks to marinade; coat well with marinade. Marinate for 12 hours, turning steaks frequently.

Drain steaks; arrange on broiler pan. Place under preheated broiler. Broil 4 minutes on each side.

Meanwhile, remove stems from tomatoes; cut off approximately ½-inch slices from bottoms. Scoop out seeds; discard. Sprinkle insides of tomatoes with salt and pepper.

Place bean sprouts and catsup into small skillet. Heat for 5 minutes. Spoon into tomatoes.

Arrange steaks on preheated serving platter. Garnish with stuffed tomatoes. Makes 4 servings.

Note: If using fresh bean sprouts, blanch, then rinse them with cold water before using.

grilled steaks

marinade

½ cup soy sauce
4 tablespoons minced onions
2 cloves garlic, minced
1 tablespoon (or less) sugar
1 tablespoon minced fresh gingerroot
¼ cup rice wine, or dry white wine

4 small steaks of your choice, boneless

Cherry tomatoes for garnish

Mix together marinade ingredients.

Pour marinade over steaks. Refrigerate overnight or let sit at room temperature for 3 to 4 hours.

Broil in the oven or on a grill or hibachi. Baste steaks with marinade while they are grilling. When steaks are almost done, grill tomatoes and use for garnish. Makes 4 servings.

marinated steak

1 to 1½ pounds filet mignon
or round steak

marinade
4 tablespoons sherry
4 tablespoons soy sauce
1½ heaping tablespoons
cornstarch
Salt
Pinch of sugar
Pinch of white pepper

4 tablespoons oil

Cut filet mignon into thin slices.

Prepare marinade by stirring sherry, soy sauce, cornstarch, a little salt, and a pinch each of sugar and white pepper thoroughly until well-blended.

Pour marinade over meat slices; marinate for 1 hour.

Heat oil in heavy skillet until very hot. Add meat, including marinade; cook for 5 minutes, stirring constantly.

Serve steak immediately. Makes approximately 4 servings.

japanese beef stew

Very good!

8 cups beef stock
3 pounds beef stew meat, cut
into bite-size pieces
4 turnips, quartered
2 carrots, cut into bite-size
pieces
2 cans water chestnuts, sliced
if desired
10 small potatoes, peeled and
left whole
Salt to taste
Freshly ground black pepper
to taste
2 tablespoons soy sauce
4 stalks celery, cut into 1-inch
pieces
10 small white onions
4 scallions, cut into ½-inch
pieces

Bring beef stock to a boil; add all ingredients except celery, white onions, and scallions. Simmer for 30 minutes, add celery and onions, and simmer until meat is tender. Add scallions; simmer for 2 minutes more.

Serve stew with rice, if desired. Makes approximately 6 servings.

beef sukiyaki

This is a recipe that we enjoy immensely. You must, however, have everything prepared prior to cooking. This is an eye-appealing dish, perfect to prepare in front of guests.

2 pounds beef sirloin, cut into strips
1 large Bermuda onion
3 stalks celery
¼ pound fresh mushrooms
12 scallions
5 ounces canned water chestnuts
¼ pound fresh spinach
1 tablespoon oil
¾ cup beef bouillon
½ cup soy sauce
¼ cup vermouth
1 tablespoon sugar

Have the butcher cut the sirloin into thin strips, or, if you are cutting it, partially freeze it to make it easier to slice.

Slice onion; put aside.

Slice the celery at an angle into thin slices. Set aside.

Thinly slice mushrooms; set aside.

Slice scallions into approximately 1½-inch pieces.

Drain the water chestnuts; slice in half.

Wash the spinach; tear it into pieces.

Arrange meat and vegetables on large platter.

Put oil into extra-large skillet or wok. Brown the meat; push to side of pan or wok. Add all vegetables except spinach; stir in bouillon, soy sauce, vermouth, and sugar. Let sizzle for 5 minutes. Add spinach, cover, and cook 2 minutes more.

Serve sukiyaki with rice. Makes 3 to 4 servings.

marinated and broiled lamb chops

These are very good!

4 lamb chops, each about 1½ inches thick

marinade

½ cup soy sauce
½ cup water
2 cloves garlic, minced
1 tablespoon freshly grated gingerroot or 1½ teaspoons ground ginger

Put lamb chops in a dish large enough to hold them and the marinade.

Mix together soy sauce, water, garlic, and ginger. Blend well.

Pour marinade over chops. Marinate overnight in refrigerator.

Let chops come to room temperature, place on broiler pan, and brush with marinade. Broil about 5 minutes, then turn and brush with additional marinade; broil for about 3 more minutes or until desired brownness is reached.

Boil and strain the remainder of the marinade. Serve it with the chops, along with rice, if desired. This can also be cooked on grill or hibachi. Makes 4 servings.

fried pork

1 medium red pepper
2 tablespoons chopped scallions
2 tablespoons ground sesame seeds
3 tablespoons soy sauce
2 tablespoons rice wine or sherry
1 pound sliced pork, ¼ inch thick
2 tablespoons oil
2 ounces transparent noodles or very thin spaghetti
1 medium cucumber, cut into thin strips
1 medium tomato, cut into thin strips

sauce
2 tablespoons vinegar
1 teaspoon freshly ground black pepper
1 tablespoon sugar

Remove seeds from pepper; dice it fine. Mix with scallions, sesame seeds, soy sauce, and rice wine or sherry. Marinate pork in this mixture for at least 1 hour.

Heat oil in frying pan. Drain pork; brown well on both sides in hot oil. Cut into smaller pieces, if desired.

Prepare noodles or thin spaghetti. Combine with cucumber and tomato strips. Place on platter along with the pork.

Prepare sauce by blending the vinegar, black pepper, and sugar.

Spoon sauce over the pork. Makes 4 servings.

skewered japanese pork

1 pound pork, cut into bite-size pieces, ½ inch thick
1 small eggplant cut into bite-size cubes
4 or 5 scallions, cut into 1½-inch lengths
2 green peppers, cut into chunks
Flour for dredging
Oil for frying

Skewer pork, eggplant, scallions, and peppers on skewers. Dredge in flour; fry in oil for about 4 minutes, or until browned. Remove from oil and, if desired, brush with soy sauce.

Serve pork with rice. Makes 2 to 3 servings.

tasty fondue

teriyaki meatballs

oriental pork and peas

marinated steak

pickled fruits

oriental pork and peas

12 ounces lean pork or tenderloin

marinade

2 tablespoons soy sauce
2 teaspoons rice wine or sherry
⅛ teaspoon monosodium glutamate (MSG)
1 egg white
1 teaspoon cornstarch
Salt
White pepper

4 ounces frozen peas
8 tablespoons oil
½ cup hot beef broth
Salt
Sugar
1 leek
1 clove garlic
1 sugared or candied ginger
4 ounces canned sliced mushrooms
4 ounces canned bamboo shoots
1 tablespoon rice wine or sherry
1 tablespoon cornstarch
2 tablespoons oyster sauce
2 teaspoons soy sauce
White pepper
Pinch of ground ginger

Cut pork or tenderloin crosswise into thin strips.

Prepare marinade by stirring together soy sauce, rice wine (or sherry), MSG, egg white, and cornstarch until well-blended. Season to taste with salt and white pepper.

Pour marinade over meat, cover, and refrigerate for 30 minutes.

In the meantime let peas thaw for 5 minutes.

Heat 2 tablespoons of the oil in a small saucepan. Add peas. Pour in beef broth; season to taste with salt and sugar. Cook for 5 minutes. Drain peas, reserving cooking liquid. Set peas aside; keep them warm.

Thoroughly clean the leek; cut it into long, thin strips.

Mince the garlic.

Cut sugared ginger into slices.

Drain mushrooms and bamboo shoots.

Heat 3 tablespoons of the oil in large saucepan. Add all vegetables and garlic; cook for 5 minutes, stirring constantly. Set aside; keep them warm.

Heat remaining oil (3 tablespoons) in skillet. Add meat strips and marinade; cook for 3 minutes, stirring constantly. Add meat and reserved peas to vegetables. Pour in rice wine (or sherry) and cooking liquid from peas. Bring to a boil.

Blend together cornstarch, oyster sauce, and soy sauce. Pour into meat –vegetable mixture; stir until smooth and bubbly. Correct seasoning, if necessary, with salt, pepper, ground ginger, and sugar.

Serve pork immediately. Makes approximately 4 servings.

skewered pork and vegetables

8 ounces pork
Salt and pepper to taste
Lima beans
Celery, cut into 1-inch pieces
Small green peppers, cut into cubes
Small onions, quartered
Fresh mushrooms, halved
Flour
Eggs, beaten
Bread crumbs
Oil for frying

sauce
2 tablespoons Worcestershire sauce
1½ tablespoons catsup

Cut meat into 1-inch chunks. Season with salt and pepper.

Prepare vegetables, using as much as is needed.

Dip meat and vegetables into flour, beaten eggs, and bread crumbs in that order, again using as much as is needed. Put meat and vegetables on skewers; fry pork over medium heat until done. Fry vegetables over high heat until browned.

Serve with sauce made from Worcestershire sauce and catsup. Makes 4 servings.

pork with peppers and tomatoes

1½ pounds lean pork
½ pound green peppers
5 ounces fresh mushrooms
½ pound tomatoes, peeled
7 tablespoons oil
Salt
¼ teaspoon ground ginger
½ pound onions
1 clove garlic
2 tablespoons sherry
1 cup hot beef broth
1 tablespoon cornstarch
4 tablespoons cold water

Cut pork and green peppers into long, thin strips.

Cut mushrooms and peeled tomatoes into thin slices.

Heat 4 tablespoons of the oil in skillet. Add green peppers, mushrooms, and tomatoes; cook for 5 minutes. Set aside.

In second skillet, heat remaining 3 tablespoons oil. Add meat; sprinkle with salt and ginger; brown, stirring constantly, for about 10 minutes.

Chop onions finely; mince garlic. Add to meat; continue cooking for another 5 minutes. Pour in sherry, beef broth, and soy sauce. Add vegetable mixture to meat; cover, and simmer for 25 minutes over medium heat.

Blend cornstarch and water; stir into skillet until smooth and bubbly.

Serve pork immediately on preheated platter. Makes 4 servings.

pickled fruits

This is delicious with cold or hot meats. Also very good with fish.

½ pound canned pineapple slices
½ pound canned apricots
½ pound canned figs
½ pound canned peaches
1¼ teaspoons allspice
1 clove (whole)
2 pieces stick cinnamon, about 4 inches long
4 tablespoons sugar
½ cup vinegar
Pinch of salt
1 small jar maraschino cherries (4 to 5 ounces)
2 jiggers brandy

Drain fruits thoroughly, reserving juices.

Place spices in a cheesecloth, tie securely, and place in saucepan together with reserved fruit juices. Add sugar, vinegar, and salt; boil for 10 minutes. Add fruits and maraschino cherries; simmer over very low heat for 1 hour. Remove cheesecloth with spices. Pour in brandy. Cover saucepan, remove from heat, and let cool. When cooled, place in refrigerator for at least 24 hours before serving. Will keep for 3 weeks when refrigerated.

chicken

japanese fried chicken

2½ to 3 pounds fryer, cut into pieces

marinade
4 tablespoons soy sauce
2 teaspoons mirin or sherry
Juice of 1 lemon
Salt
Paprika

4 tablespoons (approximately) cornstarch
Oil for frying

After cutting up chicken, wash and pat it dry.

Mix together soy sauce, mirin (if substituting sherry, add 1 teaspoon sugar), lemon juice, dash of salt, and dash of paprika.

Marinate chicken pieces in marinade for at least 2 hours; drain off excess liquid. Sprinkle chicken thoroughly with cornstarch.

Fry in oil on medium temperature for about 15 to 20 minutes, or until chicken is nicely browned. Drain on paper towels. Makes 4 servings.

chicken breasts teriyaki

2 chicken breasts, halved, boned, and skin removed
4 tablespoons oil
4 tablespoons soy sauce
4 tablespoons sugar
½ teaspoon freshly grated ginger or ¼ teaspoon ground ginger

Parboil chicken breasts for only about 30 seconds. Drain.

Heat oil medium high; brown the chicken. Pour off the oil. Add the soy sauce, sugar, and ginger to the pan; cover, and simmer until sauce is like syrup.

Serve chicken with rice, if desired. Makes approximately 2 to 3 servings.

baked chicken legs with fruit

1 teaspoon paprika
½ teaspoon ground ginger
1 teaspoon seasoned salt
¼ cup flour
6 chicken legs, disjointed, using thigh and leg
¼ cup shortening
1 29-ounce can or jar fruits-for-salad
3 oranges, peeled and cut into bite-size pieces
1 tablespoon brown sugar
2 teaspoons soy sauce
1 tablespoon cornstarch

Mix together paprika, ginger, seasoned salt, and flour. Place in small paper or double-plastic bag. Drop chicken in bag, one piece at a time, until well-coated. Set aside.

Heat shortening in skillet to low-medium heat. Brown chicken on all sides.

Tear 6 pieces of heavy-duty aluminum foil large enough to hold chicken and fruit. On each piece of foil, place 1 thigh and 1 leg.

Drain fruits, reserving liquid. Mix the canned fruit with the orange pieces; place 1/6 of fruit on each piece of foil, along with chicken pieces.

Into small saucepan place 1 cup of fruit syrup, brown sugar, soy sauce, and cornstarch. Mix well; bring to a boil. Simmer for 3 minutes. Spoon sauce over chicken and fruit. Fold foil; seal, by double-folding edges. Place packages in pan; bake at 425°F for 1½ hours or until chicken is tender. Makes 6 servings.

oriental chicken

4 ounces almonds, whole, sliced, or slivered (blanched)
3 tablespoons oil, peanut or vegetable
¾ cup chopped onion
4 chicken breasts, boned and sliced thin
2 cans sliced bamboo shoots, drained
1 can water chestnuts, drained and sliced
1 cucumber, unpeeled and thinly sliced
½ cup chicken stock
2 teaspoons sherry
¼ teaspoon ground ginger
1 teaspoon soy sauce
½ teaspoon cornstarch
1 tablespoon cold water
Salt to taste
Freshly ground pepper to taste

Brown almonds in 400°F oven for about 10 minutes. Watch closely.

Pour oil into large frying pan or wok; heat to medium-high heat. Add onion; cook it until limp. Remove onion from pan (or push up the side, if using wok). Add chicken; toss gently for about 1 minute. Add bamboo shoots and water chestnuts; toss gently for 1 minute. Add cucumber; cook for 1 minute.

Combine chicken stock, sherry, ginger, and soy sauce. Add to pan; cook for 1 minute.

Combine cornstarch and water in a small dish. Stir slowly into hot mixture. Season with salt and pepper; cook until liquid is thickened. While it is cooking, return onions to mixture.

Serve chicken with rice and the browned almonds. Makes 4 servings.

chicken with sesame seeds

This may also be made with pork or beef.

12 ounces boned chicken wings or breast meat
2 tablespoons rice wine or sherry
½ teaspoon (scant) salt
½ teaspoon oil
2 teaspoons sesame seeds

Sprinkle chicken with rice wine or sherry and salt. Set aside for 30 minutes.

Heat oil in frying pan, brown meat on both sides, and remove to preheated platter. Heat sesame seeds in frying pan; sprinkle on the chicken. Makes 2 servings.

sesame chicken

1 chicken, cut-up, about 2½ to 3 pounds
Flour mixed with salt and pepper
2 eggs, beaten
2 tablespoons milk
1 cup flour mixed with ½ cup sesame seeds, ½ teaspoon salt, and ¼ teaspoon pepper
Peanut oil for frying

cream sauce
4 tablespoons butter, melted
4 tablespoons flour
½ cup half-and-half
1 cup chicken stock
½ cup whipping cream
½ teaspoon salt or onion salt, if desired

Wash chicken; pat dry. Dust with seasoned flour.

Mix beaten eggs with milk. Dip chicken into this mixture, then roll it in the sesame-seed mixture. Fry in oil until light brown and tender.

To prepare the sauce, blend the flour into the butter over low heat, stirring constantly. Mix together the half-and-half, chicken stock, and whipping cream. Gradually add to the butter and flour, stirring constantly. When smooth, stir in the salt or onion salt.

Serve sauce immediately with the chicken. Makes 3 to 4 servings.

skewered chicken pieces

marinade
1 cup soy sauce
1 cup sake (rice wine) or sherry
3 tablespoons sugar, or little less
2 teaspoons freshly ground pepper

1½ to 2 pounds chicken meat, cut in cubes

Mix together soy sauce, sake or sherry, sugar, and pepper; bring to a boil.

Marinate the chicken in the marinade for 30 minutes, put chicken pieces on skewer, and broil; or, put on grill or hibachi. Brush with extra marinade during cooking, turning to brown well on all sides. Makes 2 servings.

chicken patties

¾ cup chopped leftover cooked chicken
2 cups mashed potatoes
2 eggs
Bread or cracker crumbs
Oil for frying

Combine chicken, potatoes, and eggs. Mix well. Roll in bread or cracker crumbs; fry in hot oil.

Dip patties in soy sauce, if desired, before enjoying. Makes 4 to 6 servings.

chicken sukiyaki

2 cups chicken stock
1 cup sugar
1 cup soy sauce
1 pound chicken meat, cut into bite-size pieces
8 large mushrooms, sliced
3 carrots, sliced diagonally and parboiled
6 scallions, cut into 2-inch lengths

Boil chicken stock that has been mixed with sugar and soy sauce. Add half of the chicken; simmer about 12 minutes. Add half of remaining ingredients; simmer another 3 minutes.

Serve this with rice, and start the process over again. Makes 2 to 3 servings.

chicken teriyaki

This is delicious served with rice that has pan drippings poured over it.

1 broiler chicken, 2½ to 3 pounds, cut up

marinade
¾ cup soy sauce
¼ cup sugar
¼ cup sherry or sake
2 teaspoons grated fresh gingerroot
1 large clove garlic, crushed

Wash chicken; pat dry.

Mix together marinade ingredients.

Place chicken in marinade. Cover and refrigerate for several hours, turning occasionally.

Drain chicken, reserving marinade. Place skin-side-down in greased baking pan. Bake in 450°F oven for 15 minutes. Turn chicken; bake for another 15 minutes. Reduce oven temperature to 350°F. Pour off and reserve liquid in pan. Continue baking for approximately 30 minutes or until chicken is tender, brushing occasionally with reserved marinade.

Broil (if desired) about 6 inches from heat until well-browned. Makes 4 servings.

sandie's chicken wings

marinade
1 10-ounce bottle soy sauce
2 teaspoons freshly grated ginger, or 1 teaspoon powdered ginger
2 cloves garlic, minced
⅓ cup brown sugar
1 teaspoon dark mustard

24 chicken wings
Garlic powder

Mix together soy sauce, ginger, garlic, brown sugar, and mustard. Blend well.

Marinate chicken wings in marinade for 2 hours or longer.

Drain wings, reserving marinade. Bake for 1½ hours at 350°F, turning and basting with marinade frequently. Sprinkle with garlic powder; place under broiler for 1 or 2 minutes just before serving to get crispy. Makes 8 to 12 servings as an appetizer, or 4 to 5 servings as a main dish.

jean's oriental chicken livers

These chicken livers are delicious!

8 ounces chicken livers, cut in half
⅓ cup soy sauce
½ cup flour
Oil for frying
1 small onion, sliced, or onion flakes

Marinate chicken livers overnight in soy sauce.

Remove livers from marinade; dredge in flour.

Heat small amount of oil in frying pan; fry livers and onions until browned.

Serve livers as an appetizer, or with rice as a main dish. Makes approximately 3 to 4 servings as an appetizer, or approximately 2 servings as a main dish.

simmered chicken livers

1 pound chicken livers
1 cup soy sauce
3 tablespoons white wine
1½ cups water
3 tablespoons sugar
1 tablespoon freshly grated ginger or ½ tablespoon ground ginger
8 scallions, cut into 1-inch pieces

Cut the chicken livers in half.

Mix together the soy sauce, wine, water, sugar, and ginger. Bring this mixture to a boil; add the livers to it. Boil slowly until most of the liquid is absorbed. Add scallions; cook for another 2 minutes. Makes 4 servings as an appetizer, or 2 servings as a main dish.

seafood

fried fish

2 eggs, beaten
2 tablespoons water
4 fish fillets
Bread or cracker crumbs
Oil for frying
Soy sauce

Beat eggs, add water, and mix together. Dip fish in egg mixture, then into bread or cracker crumbs. Fry fish in heated oil until done.

Sprinkle with soy sauce to taste, and serve with rice, if desired. Makes 4 servings.

raw fish

1 pound fresh salmon, tuna, or other fish of your choice
Handful of fresh dill, parsley, watercress, or other type of greens
2 teaspoons horseradish
4 tablespoons soy sauce

Slice fish; arrange on platter along with greens.

Mix horseradish and soy sauce; dip the fish into sauce before eating. If desired, freshly grated ginger may be substituted for the horseradish.

Capers may be used for garnish. Makes approximately 4 servings.

fish in sweet-and-sour sauce

1 to 1½ pounds fish fillet (cod, haddock, or turbot)
Juice of half a lemon
2 tablespoons soy sauce
Salt
3 tablespoons cornstarch

sweet-and-sour sauce
5 tablespoons vinegar
½ cup water
6 teaspoons sugar
3 tablespoons soy sauce
3 slices lemon
3 tablespoons cornstarch
Cold water

4 cups oil for frying

Wash fish thoroughly; pat dry. Sprinkle with lemon juice and soy sauce. Cut into 1½-inch-wide strips. Set aside for 15 minutes and let marinate. Season to taste with salt and roll in cornstarch.

To prepare sauce, bring vinegar, water, sugar, soy sauce, and lemon slices to a boil over high heat. Reduce heat to lowest point; simmer sauce for 20 minutes. Blend cornstarch with small amount of cold water; add to sauce. Stir until smooth and bubbly.

About 5 minutes before sauce is done, place fish in hot oil, and fry for about 8 minutes. Fish is done when it floats to the surface. Remove fish pieces with slotted spoon; drain on paper towels.

Arrange on serving platter and spoon sauce over fish. Serve immediately. Sauce can also be served separately. Makes approximately 3 to 4 servings.

fish teriyaki

This is a tasty, easy to prepare "something different" dish.

marinade
1 cup soy sauce
¼ cup sugar (a little more, if you prefer it sweeter)
¼ cup salad oil
2 teaspoons grated fresh gingerroot or ground ginger
1 large clove of garlic, chopped fine

1½ to 2 pounds fish fillets (rock, red snapper, ocean perch, or haddock)
1 tablespoon sesame seeds

Combine soy sauce, sugar, oil, ginger, and garlic in a bowl.

Let fish fillets marinate in marinade for 3 to 4 hours. After arranging fish on broiling pan, pour on a little of the marinade. Broil 6 inches from heat for about 4 minutes. Turn, add a little more marinade, and sprinkle fish with sesame seeds. Broil about 4 minutes longer, or until fish flakes. Makes 4 servings.

easy fish teriyaki

4 fish fillets
Soy sauce
Oil

Place fish on broiler; brush with soy sauce and oil. Broil fish, turning frequently and basting with soy sauce, until fish flakes. Makes 4 servings.

fish and vegetables in foil

4 fillets of white fish meat, about 4 ounces each
1 teaspoon salt
1 tablespoon rice wine or sherry
12 shrimp, with shells
Pepper to taste
4 fresh mushrooms
Aluminum foil, heavy duty
Salad oil
20 gingko nuts, canned (optional)

Wash fish, pat dry, and sprinkle with ½ teaspoon of the salt and the rice wine or sherry. Set aside while preparing shrimp.

Keeping the shrimp in their shells, slit the shells in the backs, and remove veins. Sprinkle with ½ teaspoon salt and pepper.

Wash mushrooms; set aside.

Brush a piece of foil (large enough to wrap the fish, shrimp, mushrooms, and gingko nuts in) with oil. Lay the fish, shrimp, mushrooms, and nuts on foil; pinch ends together to seal it.

Heat frying pan over medium heat; place foil package in pan. Cover; bake for approximately 15 minutes. Makes 4 servings.

onions and seafood in miso sauce

1 pound small onions
1 cup small clams or scallops
Vinegar for soaking clams

miso sauce

2 tablespoons sugar
2 tablespoons dashi
4 tablespoons miso
2 tablespoons vinegar

Slice the onions; boil until just tender.

Soak the clams in a small amount of vinegar while onions are boiling. If using scallops, lightly salt them before soaking in the vinegar.

Add sugar and dashi to the miso; blend very well. Stir in the vinegar.

Drain the clams or scallops; add, along with the onions, to the sauce.

Serve seafood immediately. Makes 2 servings.

japanese fish

1 whole trout, about 1 pound
1 whole carp, about 3 pounds
Juice of 1 lemon
Salt
White pepper
2 slices lean bacon
Margarine to grease pan
4 large leaves savoy cabbage (if unavailable, use regular cabbage)
1 pound fresh mushrooms
2 pieces sugared or candied ginger
3 tablespoons soy sauce
Pinch of ground anise
1 cup hot water
2 teaspoons cornstarch
Cold water
2 tablespoons bacon drippings
Juice of half a lemon

garnish
2 tablespoons chopped parsley
Lemon slices

Have fishmonger scale and clean out the insides of the fish, but leave fish whole.

At home wash fish thoroughly under running water, pat dry, and rub with lemon juice. With sharp knife make shallow incisions in backs of both fish; rub with salt and pepper.

Cut bacon into small strips; insert one strip in each incision.

Grease ovenproof baking dish with margarine; line with cabbage leaves. Place fish on top.

Slice mushrooms and sugared ginger. Mix together; spoon over fish. Sprinkle with soy sauce and ground anise. Pour in small amount of hot water. Cover with lid or aluminum foil; place in preheated 350°F oven. Bake for 30 minutes. While baking, gradually add rest of hot water, and baste fish with pan drippings. Remove fish and cabbage leaves from pan. Arrange on a preheated platter.

Bring pan drippings to a boil, scraping all brown particles from bottom of pan and adding more water, if necessary.

Blend cornstarch with small amount of cold water, add to pan drippings, and stir until sauce is smooth and bubbly. Correct seasonings, if necessary, and serve separately.

Melt and heat bacon drippings. Pour over fish and sprinkle with lemon juice.

Garnish fish with chopped parsley and lemon slices. Makes approximately 4 servings.

steamed whole fish

steamed whole fish

1½ pounds whole fish (flounder, pike, trout, or sea bass)
1 teaspoon salt
½ teaspoon freshly ground pepper
¼ teaspoon powdered ginger
3 cups water
2 teaspoons mixed pickling spices (more, if you prefer it spicier)
2 bay leaves
2 cloves garlic, cut in half
2 tablespoons chopped scallion

garnish
Lemon slices
Tomato
Parsley

Have fish scaled and cleaned and head removed, if you prefer. Lightly score the skin so seasonings will flavor the fish.

Combine salt, pepper, and ginger; rub on fish thoroughly.

Pour water into large frying pan or wok; add pickling spices, bay leaves, garlic, and scallion. Place rack in pan so that the fish will sit above the liquid, in order to allow the steam to circulate. Place the fish on the rack, cover, and let simmer for approximately 30 minutes, or until fish is tender.

Garnish fish with lemon slices, tomato, and parsley. Makes 3 servings.

cod fillets in shrimp sauce

4 cod fillets, about 6 ounces each
Juice of 1 lemon
Salt
White pepper
2 tablespoons butter
1 medium onion, sliced
2 tablespoons chopped parsley
½ cup dry white wine

shrimp sauce
2 tablespoons butter
1½ tablespoons flour
1 cup hot beef broth
½ cup dry white wine
6 ounces fresh mushrooms
4 ounces fresh shrimp
2 teaspoons lemon juice
Salt
2 egg yolks

garnish
Lemon slices
Parsley

Sprinkle cod fillets with lemon juice. Let stand for 10 minutes. Season to taste with salt and pepper.

Heat butter in large skillet. Add fish; brown well for about 10 minutes on each side. Add sliced onion; cook until golden. Stir in chopped parsley. Pour in white wine; simmer for another 5 minutes. Remove cod fillets to preheated platter; keep them warm. Reserve pan drippings.

To prepare sauce, melt butter in a saucepan. Stir in flour; pour in hot beef broth, as well as reserved pan drippings. Add white wine. Let simmer over low heat. Cut mushrooms into thin slices and add, together with shrimp, to sauce; simmer for 15 minutes. Season to taste with lemon juice and salt. Remove small amount of sauce; blend with egg yolks. Return to sauce; stir thoroughly; heat through, but do not boil, since yolks will curdle.

Pour sauce over cod fillets. Garnish with lemon slices and parsley. Makes 4 servings.

cod fillets in shrimp sauce

eel kababs

eel kababs

2 eels, about 1 pound each

marinade
¾ cup rice wine or sherry
3 teaspoons honey
5 tablespoons soy sauce

Skin eels, cut off heads, and, with a very sharp knife, remove eel fillets from bone. Cut into 1½-inch pieces; place in deep bowl.

Combine rice wine (or sherry), honey, and soy sauce. Heat.

Pour marinade over eel pieces. Let marinate for 30 minutes.

Light coals in your barbecue grill; wait until white hot. Thread eel pieces on metal skewers; place on grill. Turn skewers occasionally; baste with marinade. Grill for 15 minutes. This can also be done under the oven broiler or on a hibachi. Makes approximately 2 to 3 servings.

raw fish

japanese crab cakes

12 ounces fresh crab meat, or canned, if fresh is unavailable
1 cup frozen peas
3 eggs
1 cup chopped fresh mushrooms
1 teaspoon freshly grated ginger or ½ teaspoon ground ginger
Oil
Soy sauce for dipping

Combine crab meat, peas, eggs, mushrooms, and ginger. Mix well.

Heat oil in large frying pan; fry all the batter at once, like a pancake. Fry well on one side, then turn carefully and fry well on the other side.

Cut into slices and dip into soy sauce. Makes 3 servings.

crab-meat dumplings

12 ounces fresh crab meat, or frozen, if fresh is unavailable
3 tablespoons bread or cracker crumbs
1 egg, beaten
Flour for hands

batter
1 cup flour
1 egg
1 cup water

Oil for frying

Mix together thoroughly the crab meat, bread or cracker crumbs, and egg. Make small balls with floured hands; refrigerate for about 30 minutes.

Meanwhile make batter of flour, egg, and water; blend until well-mixed. If it remains lumpy, it's all right.

Heat oil; dip balls into batter, then fry in hot oil. Drain on paper toweling.

Serve with soy sauce, if desired. Makes 2 to 3 servings.

japanese-style tuna casserole

1 small can tuna
½ cup diced onion
½ cup diced celery
1 can bean sprouts, rinsed with cold water and drained
¼ cup diced green pepper
Soy sauce to taste

Drain tuna; mix with onion, celery, bean sprouts, green pepper, and soy sauce to taste. Place in casserole; bake at 350°F for 30 minutes. Add additional soy sauce, if needed. Makes approximately 2 to 3 servings.

broiled scallops

1 pound fresh scallops
Melted butter
Lemon juice
Freshly ground pepper (optional)
Soy sauce
Rice

Place scallops on broiler; brush with melted butter mixed with lemon juice. Sprinkle with pepper; broil just until done.

Sprinkle with soy sauce and serve with rice. Makes 2 to 3 servings.

skewered shrimp

4 large shelled shrimp

sauce
1 tablespoon (or less) salt
4 tablespoons soy sauce
¾ tablespoon rice wine or sherry
¼ teaspoon freshly grated ginger
Asparagus tips

Cut shrimp into bite-size pieces.

Make a sauce by blending together the salt, soy sauce, rice wine (sake) or sherry, and ginger.

Dip shrimp into sauce; place on skewers.

Dip the asparagus tips into the sauce, then place on skewers. Broil in oven, basting with sauce; or grill, or use hibachi. Makes 2 servings.

boiled shrimp

2 ounces cabbage, thinly sliced
8 ounces cucumbers, peeled and cut into ¼-inch cubes
8 ounces shrimp

sauce
2 teaspoons horseradish
¼ cup soy sauce

Dip cabbage quickly into boiling water; let dry.

Peel and slice cucumbers.

Boil the shrimp in salted water for about 5 minutes.

Serve the cabbage, cucumber, and shrimp in small bowls. The shrimp is dipped into a sauce made from the horseradish and soy sauce. Makes 2 servings.

boiled shrimp with bamboo shoots

2 cups boiling water
2 tablespoons mirin (sweet rice wine)
3 tablespoons soy sauce
12 shrimp, shelled and cleaned
1 pound bamboo shoots

Bring water to a boil; add mirin and soy sauce to it. If substituting sherry for the mirin, add 1 tablespoon sugar. Cook the shrimp in the mixture until done.

Cut the bamboo shoots into small pieces; cook them in the same liquid used for the shrimp.

Serve shrimp and bamboo shoots with rice. Makes 3 to 4 servings.

golden shrimp

12 large fresh shrimp

marinade
3 tablespoons soy sauce
1 tablespoon rice wine or sherry
Ginger to taste, either ground or grated gingerroot
Cornstarch

Oil for frying

Rinse shrimp.

Mix together soy sauce, rice wine or sherry, and ginger.

Marinate shrimp in the marinade for 30 minutes. Drain well. Sprinkle shrimp with cornstarch; set aside for 3 minutes.

Heat oil in deep fryer or frying pan; fry shrimp.

The shrimp may be left whole for a main course or cut into approximately 3 pieces each for an appetizer. Makes 4 servings as an appetizer or 2 servings as a main dish.

vegetables and rice

ethel's grow-your-own bean sprouts

There is nothing like growing your own bean sprouts to have them available when you desire and to know that they are fresh. It's a very simple procedure and takes very little time. All you need is a package of mung beans (bean sprouts), a quart jar, water, and a strainer.

Soak ¼ cup mung beans in a quart jar overnight. Pour off the water (use strainer if desired), and place the jar in a dark place for 3 days, rinsing the beans 3 times a day and draining them thoroughly after each rinsing. At the end of 3 days you will have ready-to-eat, home-grown bean sprouts. Refrigerate; use as needed.

frying-pan bean sprouts

2 cups fresh bean sprouts
Oil for frying, enough to cover bottom of pan
Sprinkles of soy sauce

Blanch bean sprouts in colander; rinse them with cold water. Drain well.

Heat oil in frying pan until hot. Place bean sprouts in pan; toss until heated through. Cook quickly on high heat.

Remove bean sprouts to serving plate. Sprinkle with soy sauce to taste.

If desired, chopped scallion may be added when cooking. Makes 2 servings.

cauliflower with water chestnuts and mushrooms

1 small cauliflower
2 tablespoons oil
8 mushrooms, sliced
1 cup hot chicken broth
¼ cup sliced water chestnuts
2 tablespoons soy sauce
½ teaspoon monosodium glutamate (MSG)
Salt to taste
1 tablespoon cornstarch mixed with cold water

Trim and wash cauliflower. Break into florets. If florets are large, slice them.

Heat oil in pan; gently sauté cauliflower. Add sliced mushrooms; sauté for about 30 seconds. Add chicken broth, sliced water chestnuts, soy sauce, and seasonings. Bring mixture to a boil, cover, and simmer until cauliflower is just tender, i.e. still crunchy.

Mix cornstarch with enough cold water to make a smooth paste; slowly add to cauliflower mixture, stirring constantly until thickened. Makes 4 servings.

grilled brussels sprouts

1 pint fresh Brussels sprouts
Melted butter
Lemon juice
Paprika
Freshly ground pepper (optional)

Cook Brussels sprouts as usual. Dip them in a mixture of melted butter and lemon juice; skewer them. Sprinkle with paprika and pepper; grill or put on a hibachi for only 2 or 3 minutes, or until browned. Makes 4 servings.

fresh asparagus

Delicious!

Asparagus, as many as are needed, allowing 4 to 6 per person
½ cup boiling water
½ teaspoon salt
Melted butter
Lemon juice

Cut away fibrous part of asparagus stalks. Tie together; place in a tall pot. Add boiling water and salt. Cover; cook over medium heat about 8 minutes. Do not overcook. Drain.

Pour over asparagus melted butter to which a little lemon juice has been added.

steamed wax or green beans

Fresh beans
Small amount of water
Salt
Butter

Cook beans in small amount of water in tightly covered pan about 8 minutes, or until just tender. Season with salt and butter before serving.

fresh asparagus

steamed wax or green beans

boiled corn on the cob

pickled beets

boiled corn on the cob

4 husked ears of corn
Boiling water
Pinch of sugar
Soy sauce

Plunge corn into boiling water; add a pinch of sugar. Boil for 10 to 15 minutes.

Serve corn hot, and brush with soy sauce instead of butter. The corn can be grilled instead of boiled. Makes 4 servings.

pickled beets

3 pounds beets
1 pint vinegar
½ cup sugar
1 large stick cinnamon
1 teaspoon whole allspice
6 whole cloves
1 bay leaf
Sliced onions

Cook beets until tender. Skin when cool enough. Slice and set aside.

In saucepan combine the vinegar, sugar, and the spices (which have been put into a cheesecloth bag). Bring to a boil, add the beets, and boil 10 minutes. Discard the spice bag. Add the sliced onion to the beets; fill jars. Store in refrigerator.

cooked cabbage

1 head cabbage
Oil for cooking
Soy sauce

Cut cabbage into cubes.

Heat oil to medium high; toss cabbage in oil until completely stirred. Lower heat; let cabbage cook until tender.

Sprinkle cabbage with soy sauce to taste; serve it hot. Makes approximately 4 servings.

cabbage with sesame seeds

1 head cabbage
1 tablespoon sesame seeds, toasted
Soy sauce
Sugar
Pepper

Shred cabbage. Place in pot with small amount of water; cook until just tender. Drain well. Toss with sesame seeds, soy sauce to taste, pinch of sugar, and pepper to taste. Makes approximately 4 servings.

fried eggplant

1 medium eggplant
2 eggs, beaten
Bread or cracker crumbs
Oil for frying
Soy sauce

Peel eggplant; cut it into "french-fry"-size pieces. Dip pieces of eggplant in beaten egg, then into bread or cracker crumbs. Fry in oil over medium heat, in single layer, until brown. Drain on paper towels.

Serve eggplant hot with soy sauce for dipping. Makes approximately 4 servings as an appetizer, or approximately 2 servings as a side dish.

grilled eggplant

1 eggplant
Salt
Butter, melted, or olive oil

Peel and cube eggplant. Sprinkle thoroughly with salt; let stand about 45 minutes. Rinse, drain, and pat dry. Put eggplant cubes on skewer; brush with either melted butter or olive oil. Grill, or cook on hibachi, for about 5 minutes. Makes approximately 4 servings.

stuffed eggplant

6 eggplants, small size

stuffing
½ onion, chopped
Oil, butter, or margarine
8 ounces ground chicken
½ to ¾ cup bread crumbs
½ teaspoon salt
1 tablespoon water (a little more, if necessary)
4 tablespoons grated cheese

Cornstarch
Oil for frying
Grated gingerroot
Soy sauce for dipping

Remove stem part of eggplants. Make a cut lengthwise in half, but not all the way through. Soak eggplants in salted water.

Sauté onion in a small amount of oil, butter, or margarine just until soft. Combine with chicken, bread crumbs, salt, and water. Gently mix in cheese. Divide into 6 parts.

Wipe eggplants dry. Sprinkle cut surfaces with cornstarch. Place a layer of meat mixture inside eggplant. Sprinkle a small amount of cornstarch on meat.

Heat oil in deep-frying pan; cook over medium heat until meat is well-done.

Enjoy with grated ginger and soy sauce. Makes 4 to 6 servings.

sautéed mushrooms

1 pound fresh mushrooms
1 medium onion, chopped
Oil or butter
Freshly ground pepper
Soy sauce

Slice mushrooms.

Chop onions; sauté with the mushrooms in oil or butter for about 4 minutes. Add pepper to taste, sprinkle with soy sauce, toss, and serve. Makes 3 to 4 servings.

pickled eggplant

1 large eggplant
Salt
4 tablespoons oil
4 tablespoons soy sauce
4 tablespoons sugar
4 tablespoons vinegar

Peel eggplant; slice it thin. Salt it lightly; let stand 20 minutes. Drain thoroughly.

Combine oil, soy sauce, sugar, and vinegar in a saucepan; heat to boiling. Pour over eggplant; refrigerate for at least 3 hours before serving.

This can be served as an appetizer or as a side dish. Serve it cold. Makes approximately 8 servings as an appetizer, or approximately 4 servings as a side dish.

fresh green peas

2 cups fresh green peas
2 cups boiling water
¼ teaspoon salt
6 tablespoons sugar
1 teaspoon cornstarch
Soy sauce

Add peas to boiling water. Put in salt. Bring to a boil again, reduce heat, and simmer until soft. Add sugar; simmer for 15 minutes more. Cool. If desired, thicken with cornstarch.

Before serving, add soy sauce to taste. Makes 4 servings.

pea-pod casserole

1 package frozen pea pods, boiled
1 can water chestnuts, sliced
1 can bean sprouts, or fresh bean sprouts
1 can cream of mushroom soup
1 can onion rings (optional)

Boil pea pods for 2 minutes. Drain; place in casserole dish. Place sliced water chestnuts on top of pea pods. Next, place a layer of bean sprouts. If canned bean sprouts are used, drain. If fresh are used, first blanch, then rinse with cold water and drain well. Cover with cream of mushroom soup. Bake for 15 minutes at 350°F. Place onion rings on top; heat again for about 2 or 3 minutes. Makes 4 servings.

green-pepper sauté

2 large green (or red) peppers,
cut into chunks
Boiling water
Butter or oil
Pepper
Soy sauce

Cut peppers; cook them in boiling water for about 2 minutes. Drain; sauté in butter or oil until just beginning to turn brown. Sprinkle with pepper and soy sauce. Makes 2 to 3 servings.

japanese pickles

2 large cucumbers
⅛ cup soy sauce
¼ cup vinegar
¼ cup sugar

Peel cucumbers; slice them very thin.

Mix together soy sauce, vinegar, and sugar. Pour this over the cucumber slices; mix well, gently. Refrigerate for at least 2 hours before serving. Makes approximately 4 servings.

boiled pumpkin with soy sauce

2-pound pumpkin
Pinch sugar
Soy sauce
Sherry

Cut pumpkin in half; take out seeds and fibers. Cut pumpkin meat into bite-size pieces; boil until tender. When cooked, mash until smooth; add pinch of sugar and soy sauce and sherry to taste. Makes 4 servings.

fried rice

This is an excellent recipe for using leftover rice. Use the amount of mushrooms and scallions suitable for whatever amount of rice you have. You may also add leftover chicken. Experiment putting in different ingredients and different amounts of ingredients until you discover how your family likes it best. If you like fried rice, you'll love this!

Oil, salad or peanut
Rice, chilled leftover
Mushrooms, canned or fresh
Scallion, chopped
Soy sauce
Egg, beaten

Heat oil in skillet. Add rice; drained mushrooms, if canned, or sliced, if fresh; scallion; and soy sauce. Cook over low heat about 10 to 15 minutes, stirring occasionally. Add beaten egg; cook and stir for another 2 to 3 minutes.

Serve rice with additional soy sauce.

fried rice with catsup

2 cups cooked leftover rice
½ tablespoon oil
Leftover meat or seafood, cut into small pieces
1½ tablespoons catsup (more or less, to taste)
2 tablespoons frozen or fresh peas

Heat rice in oil for 5 minutes, stirring occasionally. Add rest of ingredients; mix thoroughly, while heating, for another 3 minutes. Makes 3 to 4 servings.

chicken rice

This is a tasty, simple dish.

6 ounces chicken meat
3½ tablespoons soy sauce
2 tablespoons mirin (sweet rice wine)
4 cups chicken stock
4 cups rice

Thinly slice chicken; marinate it for 30 minutes in a sauce made from the soy sauce and mirin. If substituting sherry for the mirin, add 1 tablespoon sugar to the sauce.

Remove the chicken; mix the sauce with the chicken stock. Use this mixture, instead of water, to boil the rice in, adding a little water if necessary to thin the mixture.

Serve the rice in 4 individual bowls, with the chicken slices on top. Makes 4 servings.

dessert yams

1½ pounds yams
Oil
4 tablespoons water
4 tablespoons soy sauce
½ cup sugar
4 tablespoons sesame seeds

Peel yams; cut them into bite-size pieces (irregular shapes).

Fry yams in oil until just tender. Remove from oil.

In a saucepan combine water, soy sauce, and sugar; simmer together. Put yams into this mixture for about 2 minutes; gently mix.

Remove yams to lightly oiled serving platter. Sprinkle with sesame seeds that have been lightly toasted. Makes 3 to 4 servings.

vinegar turnips

Turnips, about 2 pounds
1 cup sugar
⅓ cup vinegar
1 cup water
3 tablespoons salt

Peel turnips; slice them very thin. Put into a bowl or, preferably, a crock.

Combine sugar, vinegar, water, and salt in saucepan; bring to a boil. Pour the mixture over the sliced turnips; mix gently, but thoroughly. Cover; refrigerate for 5 days.

stuffed zucchini

Zucchini, large size (½ zucchini per serving)

stuffing

Meat for stuffing (ground beef, ground veal, or leftover ground meat)
Salt
Pepper
Ginger
Soy sauce

Cut zucchini in half; scoop out centers. Pat dry before filling.

Mix fresh meat as for hamburgers; season well. If desired, you may add a little ground ginger and a small amount of soy sauce to meat mixture.

Fill zucchini with mixture of your choice, bake in shallow baking pan at 350°F about 45 minutes or until browned.

Serve zucchini with tomato sauce. One pound of meat will probably fill 4 to 6 halves.

stuffed zucchini

tempura

tempura cornstarch batter

1½ cups cornstarch
¾ teaspoon salt
¾ cup cold water
1 egg
Peanut or vegetable oil for frying

Blend ingredients together, but do not overmix. Dip fresh vegetables or seafood into batter, then fry in hot peanut or vegetable oil. The foods you are frying should be cut into bite-size pieces. You may use a frying pan or a wok. Makes approximately 2 servings.

tempura flour batter

2 eggs, beaten
1 cup cold water
¾ cup flour
Pinch of salt

Combine 2 beaten eggs with cold water until frothy. Blend in flour. Add salt. Blend well. Keep batter cool while using it; i.e. set it in a bowl of ice.

Use a variety of vegetables, or seafood, cut into bite-size pieces. Dip into batter and fry in hot peanut or vegetable oil in wok or frying pan. Makes approximately 2 servings.

extra-light tempura batter

1 egg, separated
½ cup sifted flour
2 tablespoons cornstarch
¼ teaspoon salt
½ teaspoon pepper
½ cup cold water

In small bowl beat egg white until stiff peaks form.

In another bowl sift together flour, cornstarch, salt, and pepper.

In a separate bowl beat egg yolk and water until frothy. Gradually add flour mixture to egg yolk and water, mixing constantly. Blend until smooth. Fold egg white into yolk mixture. Blend thoroughly. Makes approximately enough batter for frying foods for 2.

tempura dipping sauce

2 teaspoons soy sauce
¼ teaspoon salt
½ teaspoon sugar
½ cup grated white radish
2 cups dashi (broth made from dried bonito and seaweed)
1 tablespoon chopped scallions

Mix together soy sauce, salt, sugar, and grated radish. Blend in dashi, then add scallions.

This sauce can be used with any food that has been fried in a tempura batter. Makes approximately 3 to 4 servings.

shrimp tempura

more tempura sauces

Any of the following may be used for dipping the tempura-fried foods:

Grated white radish
Hot (or mild) mustard
Catsup
Soy sauce
Sweet-and-sour sauce

sweet-and-sour sauce

1 tablespoon butter
1 cup water
½ cup cider vinegar
3 tablespoons soy sauce
¼ cup sugar
1 tablespoon cornstarch
3 tablespoons sherry

Melt butter in saucepan over medium heat. Blend in water, vinegar, soy sauce, and sugar. Bring to boil. Lower heat; simmer for 10 minutes.

Make a paste of the cornstarch and sherry; slowly blend it into rest of ingredients, stirring constantly until thickened. Makes approximately 2 cups.

vegetable tempura

vegetables

Use a variety of the following, or whatever is available to you:
- **Eggplant**
- **Green pepper**
- **String beans**
- **Mushrooms**
- **Onion**
- **Potato**

tempura batter

1 egg
½ cup ice water
1 cup sifted flour

Oil for deep-frying

Slice vegetables into thin strips, keeping them separate, and set aside.

To mix batter, beat egg; add cold water and sifted flour all at once. Blend thoroughly, but do not overmix.

Heat oil in deep pan (or wok) until a drop of water dropped into oil sizzles. Dip vegetables, a few at a time, in batter, then fry them until crisp, using tongs to turn them. Take out of pan or wok with slotted spoon. Drain on paper towels.

Dip vegetables in soy sauce before enjoying. Makes approximately 2 servings.

shrimp tempura

1 pound fresh large shrimp
8 ounces bamboo shoots
4 peppers, green, red, and yellow
4 small onions
2 sugared or candied ginger

tempura batter
2 ounces rice flour
6 ounces flour
1 cup water
4 jiggers rice wine or sherry
8 egg whites

4 cups oil for frying

Rinse shrimp.

Drain bamboo shoots; cut into ½-inch pieces.

Cut green peppers into ½-inch strips.

Cut onions into thick slices; separate into rings.

Slice sugared ginger.

Arrange these ingredients in separate small bowls.

To prepare batter, place flour in a bowl. In a separate bowl combine water and rice wine or sherry and egg whites until well-blended. Gradually stir into flour to form loose batter.

Heat oil in fondue pot or wok. Each person places a shrimp or piece of vegetable on a fondue fork, dips it in batter, and deep-fries it in hot oil. Makes 4 servings.

dessert tempura

This is a fun dessert to do at the table in a fondue pot or wok.

Fruit for 4 (apples, bananas, pears)
Tempura batter
Powdered sugar

Peel fruit; cut it into chunks. Dip it into tempura batter; fry it in oil. Drain on paper towels. Sprinkle with powdered sugar. Delicious with hot tea. Makes 4 servings.

tempura ice-cream balls

Oil for frying
4 ice-cream balls frozen very, very hard (vanilla, or another flavor of your choice)
Tempura batter
Sugar and cinnamon or powdered sugar

Heat oil to medium high. Remove balls from freezer; immediately dip into tempura batter, and fry until golden brown.

Serve immediately, sprinkled with cinnamon and sugar or powdered sugar. Makes 4 servings.

desserts and tea

fresh-fruit dessert

This is an ideal dessert to enjoy after a Japanese meal. It's especially good after a dinner of Sukiyaki. Use the amount of fruit needed for the number of guests you are serving. Approximate a generous amount per person, for instance 10 to 12 pieces.

Watermelon
Cantaloupe
Bananas
Lime or lemon juice
Grapes
Strawberries
Pineapple

Cut slices of watermelon and cantaloupe into chunks.

Slice bananas into about 4 pieces each; sprinkle with lime or lemon juice to prevent darkening.

Wash grapes; leave in small bunches.

Wash and hull strawberries; leave whole.

If using fresh pineapple, cut into bite-size pieces. If canned pineapple is used, you may purchase tidbits, chunks, or slices cut into quarters.

Arrange all fruit attractively on serving platter; serve with a small bowl or pitcher of Delicious Fruit Dressing (see Index), to be poured over the fruit.

Picture on opposite page: fruit bowl

fruit bowl

1 can mandarin oranges, drained
1 apple, peeled and sliced
1 banana, sliced and sprinkled with lime or lemon juice
6 dates, cut in half
⅛ cup walnut chips

Place drained mandarin oranges in glass bowl. Combine with apple, banana, and dates. Sprinkle with walnut chips. Serve and enjoy. Makes 2 servings.

stacy's fruit kebabs

This is a nice dessert for guests to do themselves.

Pineapple chunks, canned or fresh
Bananas, cut into large pieces
Mandarin oranges
Brandied peaches, cut into halves, or large pieces
Spiced crab apples, left whole

Skewer fruits; cook on hibachi. There is an endless list of fruits suitable for this. Use the fruits that appeal to you and that are available to you. Make approximately 6 to 8 pieces of fruit per serving.

steven's rice pudding

This is not a traditional Japanese dessert, but why not? It's especially enjoyable after a lighter, less-filling meal, such as fish.

1 cup converted or long-grain rice
1 teaspoon (or less) salt
4 cups milk
3 tablespoons butter
4 tablespoons sugar
½ teaspoon vanilla
½ cup raisins (optional)

Wash and drain rice.

In top of double boiler combine rice with salt and milk; cook for 1 hour. Add butter, sugar, vanilla, and raisins; mix.

Serve hot or cold. Good with sweet cream or whipped cream. Makes approximately 6 servings.

orange-cup dessert

This is a very pretty and refreshing dessert.

Oranges with unblemished skin, as many as are needed, 1 per person
Fruit such as:
Pineapple
Orange sections
Grapefruit sections
Bananas
Maraschino cherries
Walnuts

Cut slice from top of orange so that remainder of insides may be scooped out.

Combine any of the above fruits, or others of your choice, and spoon into orange shells; refrigerate until serving time. The same thing may be done with grapefruit or bananas, as pictured. If desired, a small amount of your favorite liquer may be added to the fruit.

orange-cup dessert

delicious fruit dressing

delicious fruit dressing

This is a scrumptious sauce, delicious poured over any kind of fruit.

1 cup sugar
1 egg, well-beaten
Juice and grated rind of 1 orange, 1 lime, and 1 lemon

Combine all ingredients in saucepan; blend well. Cook over medium heat, stirring constantly, until mixture comes to a boil. Boil 1 minute. Remove from heat, cool, and store in refrigerator in covered jar.

Serve as an accompaniment to a dessert of fresh fruit. Makes approximately 1 pint.

japanese tea

Green tea
Boiling water
4 tea cups

Place a good-sized pinch of tea into teapot. You may have to experiment with the amount that is palatable for you. Add enough boiling water for 4 cups; let steep for a few minutes. Have another pot of just-boiled water on the table, so that when you pour the tea your guests may add more water, if necessary. Makes 4 cups.

index